71.10/2018

D1530546

RABBITS

MICHAELA MILLER

Contents

Heinemann Interactive Library
Des Plaines, Illinois

Wild Ones

Rabbits come in all shapes and sizes, from the big Flemish giant to the small Netherland dwarf. But whatever the size and color, they all come from wild rabbits.

baby wild rabbits

For a long time rabbits were kept just for food. About 400 years ago people started to keep them as pets.

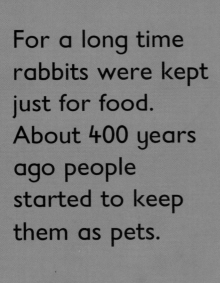

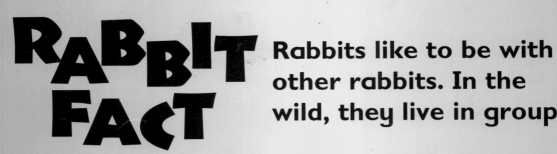

RABBIT FACT

Rabbits like to be with other rabbits. In the wild, they live in groups.

3

The Rabbit for You

Rabbits need lots of care and attention.
Before you get a rabbit, talk over it with
your whole family.

lop-eared Chinchilla rabbit

RABBIT FACT

Smaller rabbits, like Polish, Dutch, and Netherland dwarfs, are usually the best ones to choose.

Big rabbits like Flemish giants or Chinchilla gigantas are not ones to choose, unless you are big and strong yourself. They can weigh a lot and are quite a handful.

Where to Find Your Rabbit

Animal shelters are often looking for good homes for rabbits. Ask your friends and local veterinarians if they know anyone with young rabbits. Do not get a rabbit from anywhere that looks dirty.

lop-eared rabbit in a shelter

You can also buy rabbits from **breeders**. A veterinarian could let you know about local breeders. A good breeder will let you ask questions and will check that the rabbits are going to good homes.

Angora rabbit

RABBIT FACT

Long-haired rabbits, like angoras, need brushing every day.

A Healthy Rabbit

Choose a rabbit between nine and twelve weeks old that looks lively and healthy. Avoid rabbits with runny noses and signs of **diarrhea.**

RABBIT FACT

Pet rabbits which are well looked after can live up to eight years.

Your rabbit should have bright clear eyes, a sleek glossy coat, clean teeth which are not too long, and very clean ears. It should not have any cuts, lumps, or rashes.

Safe Hands

Always hold your rabbit properly. This will help it trust you. Start by turning it to face you.

Now put one hand on the **scruff** of its neck and the other hand around its rump.

Lift the rabbit toward you. Then draw your arms in so your rabbit rests closely and safely against your body.

RABBIT FACT

If your rabbit starts to struggle, it's not very happy. Put it down gently on a non-slip surface.

11

Feeding Time

Feed your rabbit two small meals at the same times each day. Lettuce, dandelions, grass, vegetables, fruit, good quality hay, and "rabbit pellets" should all be on the menu.

Rabbits need heavy feeding bowls. They will tip over light bowls.

Keep a full drip-fed water bottle with a stainless steel spout in your rabbit's home at all times. Rabbits need a small block of wood to chew on as well. This helps to keep their teeth the right length.

13

Home Sweet Home

Most pet supply store rabbit houses are too small. Your rabbit's home should be at least four feet long, two feet wide and two feet high. In some places, people keep their rabbits outside. Most people in the USA keep their rabbits inside.

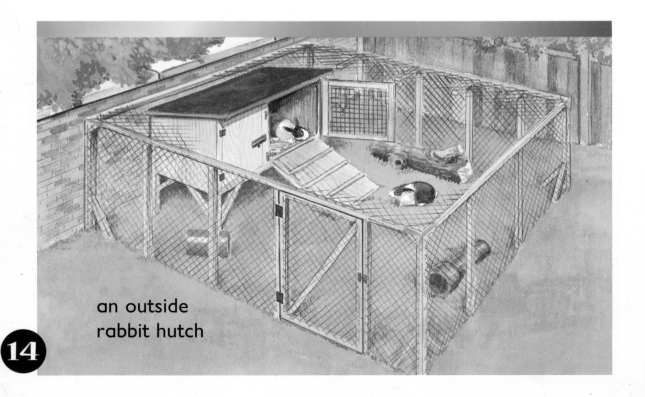

an outside
rabbit hutch

Rabbits like to hop about and graze. You can put them on a piece of grass with a strong fence around. Stay near so the rabbit is not bothered by cats or dogs.

rabbit in a burrow

RABBIT FACT

If the fence is not pushed into the ground the rabbits may burrow out.

15

Keeping Clean

Your rabbit house will need a two inch layer of sawdust, cat litter, natural wood chips, or wood shavings on the floor. A layer of straw can be placed on top. Clean the whole house twice a week.

RABBIT FACT

Wet litter and droppings must be removed every day to keep a rabbit house clean.

Rabbits can use **litter boxes** and be house-trained to live indoors with you. Try putting a few droppings and some paper soaked in its **urine** where you want it to go.

17

At the Veterinarian

Pet rabbits need to go to the veterinarian for a checkup at least once a year. Check with a veterinarian if your rabbit doesn't seem well.

If your rabbit does not want to eat, is finding breathing difficult, or has sticky ears, eyes, nose, mouth, or tail area then it needs to see a veterinarian at once.

RABBIT FACT

Baby rabbits are called kittens. They are born blind, naked, and helpless.

No More Babies

Don't let your rabbits have babies. They could have as many as eight babies per litter and two to three litters a year. It would be impossible for you to find homes for them all.

mother with her babies

RABBIT FACT

Rabbits and guinea pigs can live together if they are introduced when they are very young.

Keep rabbits of the same sex together. Male rabbits kept together need to be **neutered** to stop them fighting. Always ask your veterinarian for advice on neutering, and how to keep rabbits together.

A Note From the ASPCA

Pets are often our good friends for the very best of reasons. They don't care how we look, how we dress, or who our friends are. They like us because we are nice to them and take care of them. That's what being friends is all about.

This book has given you information to help you know what your pet needs. Learn all you can from this book and others, and from people who know about animals, such as veterinarians and workers at animal shelters, like the ASPCA. You will soon become your pet's most important friend.

MORE BOOKS TO READ

Evans, Mark. *Rabbit*. New York: Dorling Kindersley, 1992.

Zeifert, Harriet. *Let's Get a Pet*. New York: Viking, 1993.

Glossary

When words in this book are in bold, **like this**, they are explained in this glossary.

animal shelters There are lots of these shelters all around the country that look after unwanted pets and try to find them new homes.

burrow This means to dig underground. It is also the name of the underground homes of wild rabbits.

diarrhea This is a stomach upset that causes loose, or even liquid, bowel movements.

drip-fed water bottle This is a bottle which is specially made so that the water comes out drip by drip.

litter box This is a box where the rabbit can go to the bathroom. It can be filled with soil or special material called litter.

neutered This is an operation to stop rabbits being able to have babies.

scruff This is the name for the loose skin around the back of some animals' necks.

urine This is the name for liquid body waste.

23

Index

Published by Heinemann Interactive Library, an imprint of Reed Educational & Professional Publishing,
1350 East Touhy Avenue, Suite 240 West, Des Plaines, IL 60018
© 1998 RSPCA

Produced by Times Offset (M) Sdn. Bhd.
Designed by Nicki Wise and Lisa Nutt
Illustrations by Michael Strand

02 01 00 99 98
10 9 8 7 6 5 4 3 2 1

Library of Congress Cataloging-in-Publication Data
Miller, Michaela, 1961-
    Rabbits / Michaela Miller.
    p. cm. — (Pets)
    Includes bibliographical reference and index.
    Summary: A simple introduction to choosing and caring for a rabbit
as a pet.
    ISBN 1-57572-577-0 (lib. bdg.)
    1. Rabbits — Juvenile literature. [1. Rabbits. 2. Pets.]
1. Title. II. Series: Miller, Michaela. 1961- Pets.
SF453.2.M55 1998   97-11986
636.9'322—dc21   CIP
                                                            AC

Acknowledgments
The author and publishers are grateful to the following for permission to reproduce copyright photographs.
Ardea/ pp20 John Daniels; Dave Bradford pp10-13, 17, 21; Bruce Coleman Ltd p7 Fritz Prenzel; OSF/ p6 Avril Ramage, p15 G I Bernard; RSPCA/ p2 William S Paton, p3 Colin Carver, p4 E A Janes, pp5, 18, 19 Tim Sambrook, 8 A M Glue, 9 Angela Hampton;
Cover photographs reproduced with permission of: RSPCA; Dave Bradford
With special thanks to the ASPCA and their consultant Dr. Stephen Zawistowski, who approved the contents of this book.
Every effort has been made to contact copyright holders of any material reproduced in this book.
Any omissions will be rectified in subsequent printings if notice is given to the publisher.